# *This Journal* BELONGS TO

_____

_____

# DEDICATION

This Sobriety Journal Log book is dedicated to all the survivors out there who are staying sober and want to document their findings in the process.

You are my inspiration for producing books and I'm honored to be a part of keeping all of your Sobriety notes and records organized.

This journal notebook will help you record your details about staying sober.

Thoughtfully put together with these sections to record:

Number of Days Sober, What Are You Grateful For, Steps I've Taken Today To Ensure My Sobriety, How Do I Feel Today, Things I Found Hard Today, Things I Can Do To Help Tomorrow, and much more!

# HOW TO USE THIS BOOK

The purpose of this book is to keep all of your Sobriety notes all in one place. It will help keep you organized.

This Sobriety Journal will allow you to accurately document every detail about staying sober. It's a great way to chart your course through a sober you.

Here are examples of the prompts for you to fill in and write about your experience in this book:

1. Day ___ Of My Journey
2. Date/ Day/ Year, Number of Days Sober
3. What Are You Grateful For Today?
4. Steps I've Taken Today To Ensure I Stay Sober
5. How Do I Feel Today? (1-10 Rating)
6. Things I Found Hard Today
7. Things I Can Do To Help Tomorrow
8. Blank Lined Notes
9. Did You Stay Sober Today?

# Day _____ of my journey to a sober me!

| Date | Days sober |
|---|---|
|  |  |

**What are you grateful for today?**

**Steps I've taken today to ensure I stay sober**

## How did you feel today?

1  2  3  4  5  6  7  8  9  10

**Things I found hard today**

**Things I can do to help tomorrow…**

**Notes**

**Did you stay sober today?**

☐ YES  ☐ NO

# Day _____ of my journey to a sober me!

| Date | Days sober |
|---|---|
|  |  |

**What are you grateful for today?**

**Steps I've taken today to ensure I stay sober**

### How did you feel today?

# 1  2  3  4  5  6  7  8  9  10

**Things I found hard today**

**Things I can do to help tomorrow…**

**Notes**

**Did you stay sober today?**

☐ YES        ☐ NO

# Day _____ of my journey to a sober me!

| Date | Days sober |
|------|------------|

**What are you grateful for today?**

**Steps I've taken today to ensure I stay sober**

## How did you feel today?

# 1 2 3 4 5 6 7 8 9 10

**Things I found hard today**

**Things I can do to help tomorrow…**

**Notes**

**Did you stay sober today?**

☐ YES    ☐ NO

# Day _____ of my journey to a sober me!

| Date | Days sober |
|---|---|
|  |  |

**What are you grateful for today?**

**Steps I've taken today to ensure I stay sober**

### How did you feel today?

# 1  2  3  4  5  6  7  8  9  10

**Things I found hard today**

**Things I can do to help tomorrow...**

**Notes**

**Did you stay sober today?**

☐ YES    ☐ NO

# Day _____ of my journey to a sober me!

| Date | Days sober |
|---|---|
|  |  |

**What are you grateful for today?**




**Steps I've taken today to ensure I stay sober**




### How did you feel today?

1  2  3  4  5  6  7  8  9  10

**Things I found hard today**




**Things I can do to help tomorrow…**




**Notes**




**Did you stay sober today?**

☐ YES        ☐ NO

# Day _____ of my journey to a sober me!

| Date | Days sober |
|---|---|
|  |  |

**What are you grateful for today?**

**Steps I've taken today to ensure I stay sober**

### How did you feel today?

1  2  3  4  5  6  7  8  9  10

**Things I found hard today**

**Things I can do to help tomorrow...**

**Notes**

**Did you stay sober today?**

☐ YES    ☐ NO

# Day _____ of my journey to a sober me!

| Date | Days sober |
|---|---|
|  |  |

**What are you grateful for today?**



**Steps I've taken today to ensure I stay sober**



## How did you feel today?

1   2   3   4   5   6   7   8   9   10

**Things I found hard today**



**Things I can do to help tomorrow...**



**Notes**



**Did you stay sober today?**

☐ YES      ☐ NO

# Day _____ of my journey to a sober me!

| Date | Days sober |
|---|---|
|  |  |

**What are you grateful for today?**

**Steps I've taken today to ensure I stay sober**

### How did you feel today?

# 1  2  3  4  5  6  7  8  9  10

**Things I found hard today**

**Things I can do to help tomorrow…**

**Notes**

**Did you stay sober today?**

☐ YES     ☐ NO

# Day _____ of my journey to a sober me!

| Date | Days sober |
|------|------------|
|      |            |

**What are you grateful for today?**




**Steps I've taken today to ensure I stay sober**




## How did you feel today?

# 1  2  3  4  5  6  7  8  9  10

**Things I found hard today**




**Things I can do to help tomorrow…**




**Notes**




**Did you stay sober today?**

☐ YES        ☐ NO

# Day _____ of my journey to a sober me!

| Date | Days sober |
|---|---|
|  |  |

**What are you grateful for today?**

**Steps I've taken today to ensure I stay sober**

## How did you feel today?

1   2   3   4   5   6   7   8   9   10

**Things I found hard today**

**Things I can do to help tomorrow…**

**Notes**

**Did you stay sober today?**

☐ YES          ☐ NO

# Day \_\_\_\_ of my journey to a sober me!

| Date | Days sober |
|------|------------|
|      |            |

**What are you grateful for today?**

**Steps I've taken today to ensure I stay sober**

### How did you feel today?

# 1  2  3  4  5  6  7  8  9  10

**Things I found hard today**

**Things I can do to help tomorrow...**

**Notes**

**Did you stay sober today?**

☐ YES  ☐ NO

# Day _____ of my journey to a sober me!

| Date | Days sober |
|---|---|
|  |  |

**What are you grateful for today?**

**Steps I've taken today to ensure I stay sober**

## How did you feel today?

1  2  3  4  5  6  7  8  9  10

**Things I found hard today**

**Things I can do to help tomorrow…**

**Notes**

**Did you stay sober today?**

☐ YES     ☐ NO

# Day _____ of my journey to a sober me!

| Date | Days sober |
|---|---|
|  |  |

**What are you grateful for today?**

**Steps I've taken today to ensure I stay sober**

### How did you feel today?

# 1  2  3  4  5  6  7  8  9  10

**Things I found hard today**

**Things I can do to help tomorrow...**

**Notes**

**Did you stay sober today?**

☐ YES    ☐ NO

# Day _____ of my journey to a sober me!

| Date | Days sober |
|---|---|
|  |  |

**What are you grateful for today?**



**Steps I've taken today to ensure I stay sober**



## How did you feel today?

**1  2  3  4  5  6  7  8  9  10**

**Things I found hard today**



**Things I can do to help tomorrow…**



**Notes**



**Did you stay sober today?**

☐ YES        ☐ NO

# Day _____ of my journey to a sober me!

| Date | Days sober |
|---|---|
|  |  |

**What are you grateful for today?**

**Steps I've taken today to ensure I stay sober**

### How did you feel today?

# 1  2  3  4  5  6  7  8  9  10

**Things I found hard today**

**Things I can do to help tomorrow…**

**Notes**

**Did you stay sober today?**

☐ YES    ☐ NO

# Day _____ of my journey to a sober me!

| Date | Days sober |
|---|---|
|  |  |

**What are you grateful for today?**

**Steps I've taken today to ensure I stay sober**

### How did you feel today?

1   2   3   4   5   6   7   8   9   10

**Things I found hard today**

**Things I can do to help tomorrow...**

**Notes**

**Did you stay sober today?**

☐ YES    ☐ NO

# Day _____ of my journey to a sober me!

| Date | Days sober |
|---|---|
|  |  |

**What are you grateful for today?**

**Steps I've taken today to ensure I stay sober**

### How did you feel today?

**1  2  3  4  5  6  7  8  9  10**

**Things I found hard today**

**Things I can do to help tomorrow…**

**Notes**

**Did you stay sober today?**

☐ YES  ☐ NO

# Day _____ of my journey to a sober me!

| Date | Days sober |
|---|---|
| | |

**What are you grateful for today?**

**Steps I've taken today to ensure I stay sober**

### How did you feel today?

# 1  2  3  4  5  6  7  8  9  10

**Things I found hard today**

**Things I can do to help tomorrow...**

**Notes**

**Did you stay sober today?**

☐ YES    ☐ NO

# Day _____ of my journey to a sober me!

| Date | Days sober |
|------|------------|
|      |            |

**What are you grateful for today?**




**Steps I've taken today to ensure I stay sober**




### How did you feel today?

# 1  2  3  4  5  6  7  8  9  10

**Things I found hard today**




**Things I can do to help tomorrow...**




**Notes**




**Did you stay sober today?**

☐ YES          ☐ NO

# Day _____ of my journey to a sober me!

| Date | Days sober |
|---|---|

**What are you grateful for today?**

**Steps I've taken today to ensure I stay sober**

### How did you feel today?

# 1  2  3  4  5  6  7  8  9  10

**Things I found hard today**

**Things I can do to help tomorrow...**

**Notes**

**Did you stay sober today?**

☐ YES  ☐ NO

# Day _____ of my journey to a sober me!

| Date | Days sober |
|---|---|
|  |  |

**What are you grateful for today?**

**Steps I've taken today to ensure I stay sober**

**How did you feel today?**

1    2    3    4    5    6    7    8    9    10

**Things I found hard today**

**Things I can do to help tomorrow...**

**Notes**

**Did you stay sober today?**

☐ YES          ☐ NO

# Day _____ of my journey to a sober me!

| Date | Days sober |
|---|---|
|  |  |

**What are you grateful for today?**

**Steps I've taken today to ensure I stay sober**

### How did you feel today?

**1  2  3  4  5  6  7  8  9  10**

**Things I found hard today**

**Things I can do to help tomorrow...**

**Notes**

**Did you stay sober today?**

☐ YES  ☐ NO

# Day _____ of my journey to a sober me!

| Date | Days sober |
|------|------------|

**What are you grateful for today?**

**Steps I've taken today to ensure I stay sober**

### How did you feel today?

1  2  3  4  5  6  7  8  9  10

**Things I found hard today**

**Things I can do to help tomorrow...**

**Notes**

**Did you stay sober today?**

☐ YES    ☐ NO

# Day _____ of my journey to a sober me!

| Date | Days sober |
|---|---|
|  |  |

**What are you grateful for today?**

**Steps I've taken today to ensure I stay sober**

## How did you feel today?

# 1  2  3  4  5  6  7  8  9  10

**Things I found hard today**

**Things I can do to help tomorrow...**

**Notes**

**Did you stay sober today?**

☐ **YES**     ☐ **NO**

# Day _____ of my journey to a sober me!

| Date | Days sober |
|---|---|
|  |  |

**What are you grateful for today?**

**Steps I've taken today to ensure I stay sober**

### How did you feel today?

1　2　3　4　5　6　7　8　9　10

**Things I found hard today**

**Things I can do to help tomorrow…**

**Notes**

**Did you stay sober today?**

☐ YES　　☐ NO

# Day _____ of my journey to a sober me!

| Date | Days sober |
|---|---|
|  |  |

**What are you grateful for today?**




**Steps I've taken today to ensure I stay sober**




## How did you feel today?

# 1  2  3  4  5  6  7  8  9  10

**Things I found hard today**




**Things I can do to help tomorrow…**




**Notes**




**Did you stay sober today?**

☐ **YES**       ☐ **NO**

# Day _____ of my journey to a sober me!

| Date | Days sober |
|------|------------|

**What are you grateful for today?**

**Steps I've taken today to ensure I stay sober**

### How did you feel today?

# 1   2   3   4   5   6   7   8   9   10

**Things I found hard today**

**Things I can do to help tomorrow...**

**Notes**

**Did you stay sober today?**

☐ YES    ☐ NO

# Day _____ of my journey to a sober me!

| Date | Days sober |
|---|---|
|  |  |

**What are you grateful for today?**

**Steps I've taken today to ensure I stay sober**

### How did you feel today?

1   2   3   4   5   6   7   8   9   10

**Things I found hard today**

**Things I can do to help tomorrow…**

**Notes**

**Did you stay sober today?**

☐ YES     ☐ NO

# Day _____ of my journey to a sober me!

| Date | Days sober |
|---|---|
|  |  |

**What are you grateful for today?**




**Steps I've taken today to ensure I stay sober**




**How did you feel today?**

1  2  3  4  5  6  7  8  9  10

**Things I found hard today**




**Things I can do to help tomorrow…**




**Notes**




**Did you stay sober today?**

☐ YES         ☐ NO

# Day _____ of my journey to a sober me!

| Date | Days sober |
|---|---|
|  |  |

**What are you grateful for today?**



**Steps I've taken today to ensure I stay sober**



## How did you feel today?

1   2   3   4   5   6   7   8   9   10

**Things I found hard today**



**Things I can do to help tomorrow...**



**Notes**



**Did you stay sober today?**

☐ YES     ☐ NO

# Day _____ of my journey to a sober me!

| Date | Days sober |
|---|---|
|   |   |

**What are you grateful for today?**



**Steps I've taken today to ensure I stay sober**



### How did you feel today?

1   2   3   4   5   6   7   8   9   10

**Things I found hard today**



**Things I can do to help tomorrow…**



**Notes**



**Did you stay sober today?**

☐ YES    ☐ NO

# Day _____ of my journey to a sober me!

| Date | Days sober |
|---|---|
|  |  |

**What are you grateful for today?**



**Steps I've taken today to ensure I stay sober**



## How did you feel today?

# 1  2  3  4  5  6  7  8  9  10

**Things I found hard today**



**Things I can do to help tomorrow…**



**Notes**



**Did you stay sober today?**

☐ YES     ☐ NO

# Day _____ of my journey to a sober me!

| Date | Days sober |
|---|---|
|  |  |

**What are you grateful for today?**



**Steps I've taken today to ensure I stay sober**



### How did you feel today?

1    2    3    4    5    6    7    8    9    10

**Things I found hard today**



**Things I can do to help tomorrow…**



**Notes**



**Did you stay sober today?**

☐ YES           ☐ NO

# Day _____ of my journey to a sober me!

| Date | Days sober |
|---|---|
|  |  |

**What are you grateful for today?**

**Steps I've taken today to ensure I stay sober**

### How did you feel today?

1    2    3    4    5    6    7    8    9    10

**Things I found hard today**

**Things I can do to help tomorrow...**

**Notes**

**Did you stay sober today?**
☐ YES        ☐ NO

# Day _____ of my journey to a sober me!

| Date | Days sober |
|---|---|
|   |   |

**What are you grateful for today?**

**Steps I've taken today to ensure I stay sober**

### How did you feel today?

# 1　2　3　4　5　6　7　8　9　10

**Things I found hard today**

**Things I can do to help tomorrow...**

**Notes**

**Did you stay sober today?**

☐ YES        ☐ NO

# Day _____ of my journey to a sober me!

| Date | Days sober |
|---|---|
|  |  |

**What are you grateful for today?**

**Steps I've taken today to ensure I stay sober**

### How did you feel today?

# 1  2  3  4  5  6  7  8  9  10

**Things I found hard today**

**Things I can do to help tomorrow...**

**Notes**

**Did you stay sober today?**

☐ **YES**        ☐ **NO**

# Day _____ of my journey to a sober me!

| Date | Days sober |
|---|---|
|  |  |

**What are you grateful for today?**



**Steps I've taken today to ensure I stay sober**



### How did you feel today?

# 1  2  3  4  5  6  7  8  9  10

**Things I found hard today**



**Things I can do to help tomorrow…**



**Notes**



**Did you stay sober today?**

☐ YES    ☐ NO

# Day _____ of my journey to a sober me!

| Date | Days sober |
|---|---|
|  |  |

**What are you grateful for today?**

**Steps I've taken today to ensure I stay sober**

### How did you feel today?

1   2   3   4   5   6   7   8   9   10

**Things I found hard today**

**Things I can do to help tomorrow...**

**Notes**

**Did you stay sober today?**

☐ YES     ☐ NO

# Day _____ of my journey to a sober me!

| Date | Days sober |
|---|---|
|  |  |

**What are you grateful for today?**

**Steps I've taken today to ensure I stay sober**

## How did you feel today?

# 1  2  3  4  5  6  7  8  9  10

**Things I found hard today**

**Things I can do to help tomorrow...**

**Notes**

**Did you stay sober today?**

☐ YES    ☐ NO

# Day _____ of my journey to a sober me!

| Date | Days sober |
|---|---|
|  |  |

**What are you grateful for today?**



**Steps I've taken today to ensure I stay sober**



### How did you feel today?

1  2  3  4  5  6  7  8  9  10

**Things I found hard today**



**Things I can do to help tomorrow…**



**Notes**



**Did you stay sober today?**

☐ YES    ☐ NO

# Day _____ of my journey to a sober me!

| Date | Days sober |
|---|---|
|  |  |

**What are you grateful for today?**



**Steps I've taken today to ensure I stay sober**



**How did you feel today?**

1  2  3  4  5  6  7  8  9  10

**Things I found hard today**



**Things I can do to help tomorrow...**



**Notes**



**Did you stay sober today?**

☐ YES     ☐ NO

# Day _____ of my journey to a sober me!

| Date | Days sober |
|------|------------|
|      |            |

**What are you grateful for today?**

**Steps I've taken today to ensure I stay sober**

### How did you feel today?

# 1  2  3  4  5  6  7  8  9  10

**Things I found hard today**

**Things I can do to help tomorrow...**

**Notes**

**Did you stay sober today?**

☐ YES ☐ NO

# Day _____ of my journey to a sober me!

| Date | Days sober |
|---|---|
|  |  |

**What are you grateful for today?**

**Steps I've taken today to ensure I stay sober**

## How did you feel today?

1  2  3  4  5  6  7  8  9  10

**Things I found hard today**

**Things I can do to help tomorrow...**

**Notes**

**Did you stay sober today?**

☐ YES   ☐ NO

# Day _____ of my journey to a sober me!

| Date | Days sober |
|---|---|
|  |  |

**What are you grateful for today?**



**Steps I've taken today to ensure I stay sober**



### How did you feel today?

# 1  2  3  4  5  6  7  8  9  10

**Things I found hard today**



**Things I can do to help tomorrow…**



**Notes**



**Did you stay sober today?**

☐ YES     ☐ NO

# Day _____ of my journey to a sober me!

| Date | Days sober |
|---|---|
|  |  |

**What are you grateful for today?**

**Steps I've taken today to ensure I stay sober**

### How did you feel today?

# 1  2  3  4  5  6  7  8  9  10

**Things I found hard today**

**Things I can do to help tomorrow...**

**Notes**

**Did you stay sober today?**

☐ YES    ☐ NO

# Day _____ of my journey to a sober me!

| Date | Days sober |
|---|---|
|  |  |

**What are you grateful for today?**

**Steps I've taken today to ensure I stay sober**

**How did you feel today?**

1   2   3   4   5   6   7   8   9   10

**Things I found hard today**

**Things I can do to help tomorrow...**

**Notes**

**Did you stay sober today?**

☐ YES          ☐ NO

# Day _____ of my journey to a sober me!

| Date | Days sober |
|---|---|
|  |  |

**What are you grateful for today?**



**Steps I've taken today to ensure I stay sober**



## How did you feel today?

**1   2   3   4   5   6   7   8   9   10**

**Things I found hard today**



**Things I can do to help tomorrow...**



**Notes**



**Did you stay sober today?**

☐ YES          ☐ NO

# Day _____ of my journey to a sober me!

| Date | Days sober |
|---|---|
|  |  |

**What are you grateful for today?**

**Steps I've taken today to ensure I stay sober**

## How did you feel today?

1    2    3    4    5    6    7    8    9    10

**Things I found hard today**

**Things I can do to help tomorrow...**

**Notes**

**Did you stay sober today?**

☐ YES     ☐ NO

# Day _____ of my journey to a sober me!

| Date | Days sober |
|---|---|
|  |  |

**What are you grateful for today?**



**Steps I've taken today to ensure I stay sober**



## How did you feel today?

1  2  3  4  5  6  7  8  9  10

**Things I found hard today**



**Things I can do to help tomorrow...**



**Notes**



**Did you stay sober today?**

☐ YES            ☐ NO

# Day _____ of my journey to a sober me!

| Date | Days sober |
|------|------------|
|      |            |

**What are you grateful for today?**

**Steps I've taken today to ensure I stay sober**

### How did you feel today?

# 1  2  3  4  5  6  7  8  9  10

**Things I found hard today**

**Things I can do to help tomorrow…**

**Notes**

**Did you stay sober today?**

☐ YES  ☐ NO

# Day _____ of my journey to a sober me!

| Date | Days sober |
|---|---|
|  |  |

**What are you grateful for today?**

**Steps I've taken today to ensure I stay sober**

### How did you feel today?

# 1  2  3  4  5  6  7  8  9  10

**Things I found hard today**

**Things I can do to help tomorrow…**

**Notes**

**Did you stay sober today?**

☐ YES       ☐ NO

# Day _____ of my journey to a sober me!

| Date | Days sober |
|---|---|
|  |  |

**What are you grateful for today?**

**Steps I've taken today to ensure I stay sober**

## How did you feel today?

1　2　3　4　5　6　7　8　9　10

**Things I found hard today**

**Things I can do to help tomorrow…**

**Notes**

**Did you stay sober today?**

☐ YES　　☐ NO

# Day _____ of my journey to a sober me!

| Date | Days sober |
|------|------------|
|      |            |

**What are you grateful for today?**

**Steps I've taken today to ensure I stay sober**

## How did you feel today?

1   2   3   4   5   6   7   8   9   10

**Things I found hard today**

**Things I can do to help tomorrow...**

**Notes**

**Did you stay sober today?**

☐ YES ☐ NO

# Day _____ of my journey to a sober me!

| Date | Days sober |
|---|---|
|  |  |

**What are you grateful for today?**

**Steps I've taken today to ensure I stay sober**

### How did you feel today?

1  2  3  4  5  6  7  8  9  10

**Things I found hard today**

**Things I can do to help tomorrow…**

**Notes**

**Did you stay sober today?**

☐ YES ☐ NO

# Day _____ of my journey to a sober me!

| Date | Days sober |
|---|---|
|  |  |

**What are you grateful for today?**




**Steps I've taken today to ensure I stay sober**




## How did you feel today?

1   2   3   4   5   6   7   8   9   10

**Things I found hard today**




**Things I can do to help tomorrow...**




**Notes**




**Did you stay sober today?**

☐ YES     ☐ NO

# Day _____ of my journey to a sober me!

| Date | Days sober |
|---|---|
|  |  |

**What are you grateful for today?**

**Steps I've taken today to ensure I stay sober**

### How did you feel today?

**1  2  3  4  5  6  7  8  9  10**

**Things I found hard today**

**Things I can do to help tomorrow...**

**Notes**

**Did you stay sober today?**

☐ YES     ☐ NO

# Day \_\_\_\_ of my journey to a sober me!

| Date | Days sober |
|---|---|
| | |

**What are you grateful for today?**

**Steps I've taken today to ensure I stay sober**

### How did you feel today?

# 1  2  3  4  5  6  7  8  9  10

**Things I found hard today**

**Things I can do to help tomorrow…**

**Notes**

**Did you stay sober today?**

☐ **YES**   ☐ **NO**

# Day _____ of my journey to a sober me!

| Date | Days sober |
|---|---|
|  |  |

**What are you grateful for today?**

**Steps I've taken today to ensure I stay sober**

### How did you feel today?

# 1  2  3  4  5  6  7  8  9  10

**Things I found hard today**

**Things I can do to help tomorrow...**

**Notes**

**Did you stay sober today?**

☐ YES  ☐ NO

# Day _____ of my journey to a sober me!

| Date | Days sober |
|------|------------|
|      |            |

**What are you grateful for today?**

**Steps I've taken today to ensure I stay sober**

### How did you feel today?

# 1  2  3  4  5  6  7  8  9  10

**Things I found hard today**

**Things I can do to help tomorrow…**

**Notes**

**Did you stay sober today?**

☐ YES  ☐ NO

# Day _____ of my journey to a sober me!

| Date | Days sober |
|---|---|
|  |  |

**What are you grateful for today?**

**Steps I've taken today to ensure I stay sober**

### How did you feel today?

# 1  2  3  4  5  6  7  8  9  10

**Things I found hard today**

**Things I can do to help tomorrow...**

**Notes**

**Did you stay sober today?**

☐ YES  ☐ NO

# Day _____ of my journey to a sober me!

| Date | Days sober |
|---|---|
|  |  |

**What are you grateful for today?**

**Steps I've taken today to ensure I stay sober**

### How did you feel today?

1  2  3  4  5  6  7  8  9  10

**Things I found hard today**

**Things I can do to help tomorrow...**

**Notes**

**Did you stay sober today?**

☐ YES        ☐ NO

# Day _____ of my journey to a sober me!

| Date | Days sober |
|---|---|
| | |

**What are you grateful for today?**

**Steps I've taken today to ensure I stay sober**

### How did you feel today?

1  2  3  4  5  6  7  8  9  10

**Things I found hard today**

**Things I can do to help tomorrow…**

**Notes**

**Did you stay sober today?**

☐ YES    ☐ NO

# Day _____ of my journey to a sober me!

| Date | Days sober |
|---|---|
|  |  |

**What are you grateful for today?**

**Steps I've taken today to ensure I stay sober**

## How did you feel today?

1  2  3  4  5  6  7  8  9  10

**Things I found hard today**

**Things I can do to help tomorrow…**

**Notes**

**Did you stay sober today?**

☐ YES　　☐ NO

# Day _____ of my journey to a sober me!

| Date | Days sober |
|---|---|
|  |  |

**What are you grateful for today?**

**Steps I've taken today to ensure I stay sober**

### How did you feel today?

1   2   3   4   5   6   7   8   9   10

**Things I found hard today**

**Things I can do to help tomorrow...**

**Notes**

**Did you stay sober today?**

☐ YES　　☐ NO

# Day _____ of my journey to a sober me!

| Date | Days sober |
|---|---|
|  |  |

**What are you grateful for today?**


**Steps I've taken today to ensure I stay sober**


### How did you feel today?

1   2   3   4   5   6   7   8   9   10

**Things I found hard today**


**Things I can do to help tomorrow...**


**Notes**


**Did you stay sober today?**

☐ YES          ☐ NO

# Day _____ of my journey to a sober me!

| Date | Days sober |
|---|---|
|  |  |

**What are you grateful for today?**

**Steps I've taken today to ensure I stay sober**

### How did you feel today?

1    2    3    4    5    6    7    8    9    10

**Things I found hard today**

**Things I can do to help tomorrow...**

**Notes**

**Did you stay sober today?**

☐ YES        ☐ NO

# Day _____ of my journey to a sober me!

| Date | Days sober |
|------|------------|
|      |            |

**What are you grateful for today?**

**Steps I've taken today to ensure I stay sober**

### How did you feel today?

# 1  2  3  4  5  6  7  8  9  10

**Things I found hard today**

**Things I can do to help tomorrow...**

**Notes**

**Did you stay sober today?**

☐ YES          ☐ NO

# Day _____ of my journey to a sober me!

| Date | Days sober |
|------|------------|

**What are you grateful for today?**

**Steps I've taken today to ensure I stay sober**

## How did you feel today?

1  2  3  4  5  6  7  8  9  10

**Things I found hard today**

**Things I can do to help tomorrow...**

**Notes**

**Did you stay sober today?**

☐ YES    ☐ NO

# Day _____ of my journey to a sober me!

| Date | Days sober |
|---|---|
|  |  |

**What are you grateful for today?**



**Steps I've taken today to ensure I stay sober**



### How did you feel today?

# 1  2  3  4  5  6  7  8  9  10

**Things I found hard today**



**Things I can do to help tomorrow…**



**Notes**



**Did you stay sober today?**

☐ YES    ☐ NO

# Day _____ of my journey to a sober me!

| Date | Days sober |
|---|---|
|  |  |

**What are you grateful for today?**

**Steps I've taken today to ensure I stay sober**

## How did you feel today?

# 1   2   3   4   5   6   7   8   9   10

**Things I found hard today**

**Things I can do to help tomorrow…**

**Notes**

**Did you stay sober today?**

☐ YES     ☐ NO

# Day _____ of my journey to a sober me!

| Date | Days sober |
|---|---|
|  |  |

**What are you grateful for today?**

**Steps I've taken today to ensure I stay sober**

### How did you feel today?

1　2　3　4　5　6　7　8　9　10

**Things I found hard today**

**Things I can do to help tomorrow...**

**Notes**

**Did you stay sober today?**

☐ YES　　　☐ NO

# Day _____ of my journey to a sober me!

| Date | Days sober |
|---|---|
|  |  |

**What are you grateful for today?**

**Steps I've taken today to ensure I stay sober**

## How did you feel today?

# 1  2  3  4  5  6  7  8  9  10

**Things I found hard today**

**Things I can do to help tomorrow…**

**Notes**

**Did you stay sober today?**

☐ YES ☐ NO

# Day _____ of my journey to a sober me!

| Date | Days sober |
|---|---|
|  |  |

**What are you grateful for today?**

**Steps I've taken today to ensure I stay sober**

## How did you feel today?

1  2  3  4  5  6  7  8  9  10

**Things I found hard today**

**Things I can do to help tomorrow…**

**Notes**

**Did you stay sober today?**

☐ YES   ☐ NO

# Day _____ of my journey to a sober me!

| Date | Days sober |
|---|---|
|  |  |

**What are you grateful for today?**



**Steps I've taken today to ensure I stay sober**



## How did you feel today?

# 1  2  3  4  5  6  7  8  9  10

**Things I found hard today**



**Things I can do to help tomorrow…**



**Notes**



**Did you stay sober today?**

☐ YES     ☐ NO

# Day _____ of my journey to a sober me!

| Date | Days sober |
|---|---|
|  |  |

**What are you grateful for today?**

**Steps I've taken today to ensure I stay sober**

### How did you feel today?

1   2   3   4   5   6   7   8   9   10

**Things I found hard today**

**Things I can do to help tomorrow…**

**Notes**

**Did you stay sober today?**

☐ YES          ☐ NO

# Day _____ of my journey to a sober me!

| Date | Days sober |
|---|---|
|  |  |

**What are you grateful for today?**

**Steps I've taken today to ensure I stay sober**

## How did you feel today?

**1  2  3  4  5  6  7  8  9  10**

**Things I found hard today**

**Things I can do to help tomorrow...**

**Notes**

**Did you stay sober today?**

☐ YES    ☐ NO

# Day _____ of my journey to a sober me!

| Date | Days sober |
|---|---|
|  |  |

**What are you grateful for today?**

**Steps I've taken today to ensure I stay sober**

### How did you feel today?

1  2  3  4  5  6  7  8  9  10

**Things I found hard today**

**Things I can do to help tomorrow…**

**Notes**

**Did you stay sober today?**

☐ YES    ☐ NO

# Day _____ of my journey to a sober me!

| Date | Days sober |
|---|---|
|  |  |

**What are you grateful for today?**

**Steps I've taken today to ensure I stay sober**

## How did you feel today?

# 1　2　3　4　5　6　7　8　9　10

**Things I found hard today**

**Things I can do to help tomorrow…**

**Notes**

**Did you stay sober today?**

☐ YES    ☐ NO

# Day _____ of my journey to a sober me!

| Date | Days sober |
|---|---|
|  |  |

**What are you grateful for today?**

**Steps I've taken today to ensure I stay sober**

### How did you feel today?

# 1  2  3  4  5  6  7  8  9  10

**Things I found hard today**

**Things I can do to help tomorrow...**

**Notes**

**Did you stay sober today?**

☐ YES     ☐ NO

# Day _____ of my journey to a sober me!

| Date | Days sober |
|---|---|
|  |  |

**What are you grateful for today?**

**Steps I've taken today to ensure I stay sober**

### How did you feel today?

1  2  3  4  5  6  7  8  9  10

**Things I found hard today**

**Things I can do to help tomorrow…**

**Notes**

**Did you stay sober today?**

☐ YES    ☐ NO

# Day _____ of my journey to a sober me!

| Date | Days sober |
|---|---|

**What are you grateful for today?**

**Steps I've taken today to ensure I stay sober**

## How did you feel today?

# 1 2 3 4 5 6 7 8 9 10

**Things I found hard today**

**Things I can do to help tomorrow…**

**Notes**

**Did you stay sober today?**

☐ YES ☐ NO

# Day _____ of my journey to a sober me!

| Date | Days sober |
|---|---|
| | |

**What are you grateful for today?**


**Steps I've taken today to ensure I stay sober**


### How did you feel today?

1   2   3   4   5   6   7   8   9   10

**Things I found hard today**


**Things I can do to help tomorrow...**


**Notes**


**Did you stay sober today?**

☐ YES    ☐ NO

# Day _____ of my journey to a sober me!

| Date | Days sober |
|---|---|
|  |  |

**What are you grateful for today?**

**Steps I've taken today to ensure I stay sober**

## How did you feel today?

1  2  3  4  5  6  7  8  9  10

**Things I found hard today**

**Things I can do to help tomorrow...**

**Notes**

**Did you stay sober today?**

☐ YES     ☐ NO

# Day _____ of my journey to a sober me!

| Date | Days sober |
|---|---|
|  |  |

**What are you grateful for today?**

**Steps I've taken today to ensure I stay sober**

### How did you feel today?

1  2  3  4  5  6  7  8  9  10

**Things I found hard today**

**Things I can do to help tomorrow…**

**Notes**

**Did you stay sober today?**

☐ YES    ☐ NO

# Day _____ of my journey to a sober me!

| Date | Days sober |
|---|---|
|  |  |

**What are you grateful for today?**

**Steps I've taken today to ensure I stay sober**

### How did you feel today?

1  2  3  4  5  6  7  8  9  10

**Things I found hard today**

**Things I can do to help tomorrow...**

**Notes**

**Did you stay sober today?**

☐ YES    ☐ NO

# Day _____ of my journey to a sober me!

| Date | Days sober |
|---|---|
|  |  |

**What are you grateful for today?**



**Steps I've taken today to ensure I stay sober**



## How did you feel today?

1   2   3   4   5   6   7   8   9   10

**Things I found hard today**



**Things I can do to help tomorrow...**



**Notes**



**Did you stay sober today?**

☐ YES        ☐ NO

# Day _____ of my journey to a sober me!

| Date | Days sober |
|---|---|
|  |  |

**What are you grateful for today?**

**Steps I've taken today to ensure I stay sober**

### How did you feel today?

1   2   3   4   5   6   7   8   9   10

**Things I found hard today**

**Things I can do to help tomorrow...**

**Notes**

**Did you stay sober today?**

☐ YES          ☐ NO

# Day _____ of my journey to a sober me!

| Date | Days sober |
|---|---|
|  |  |

**What are you grateful for today?**


**Steps I've taken today to ensure I stay sober**


## How did you feel today?

1    2    3    4    5    6    7    8    9    10

**Things I found hard today**


**Things I can do to help tomorrow...**


**Notes**


**Did you stay sober today?**

☐ YES      ☐ NO

# Day _____ of my journey to a sober me!

| Date | Days sober |
|------|------------|

**What are you grateful for today?**

**Steps I've taken today to ensure I stay sober**

## How did you feel today?

# 1   2   3   4   5   6   7   8   9   10

**Things I found hard today**

**Things I can do to help tomorrow…**

**Notes**

**Did you stay sober today?**

☐ YES     ☐ NO

# Day _____ of my journey to a sober me!

| Date | Days sober |
|---|---|
|   |   |

**What are you grateful for today?**


**Steps I've taken today to ensure I stay sober**


### How did you feel today?

# 1  2  3  4  5  6  7  8  9  10

**Things I found hard today**


**Things I can do to help tomorrow…**


**Notes**


**Did you stay sober today?**

☐ YES    ☐ NO

# Day _____ of my journey to a sober me!

| Date | Days sober |
|---|---|
|   |   |

**What are you grateful for today?**




**Steps I've taken today to ensure I stay sober**




### How did you feel today?

# 1  2  3  4  5  6  7  8  9  10

**Things I found hard today**




**Things I can do to help tomorrow...**




**Notes**




**Did you stay sober today?**

☐ YES      ☐ NO

# Day _____ of my journey to a sober me!

| Date | Days sober |
|---|---|
| | |

**What are you grateful for today?**

**Steps I've taken today to ensure I stay sober**

## How did you feel today?

1  2  3  4  5  6  7  8  9  10

**Things I found hard today**

**Things I can do to help tomorrow...**

**Notes**

**Did you stay sober today?**

☐ YES  ☐ NO

# Day _____ of my journey to a sober me!

| Date | Days sober |
|---|---|
|  |  |

**What are you grateful for today?**



**Steps I've taken today to ensure I stay sober**



## How did you feel today?

**1   2   3   4   5   6   7   8   9   10**

**Things I found hard today**



**Things I can do to help tomorrow…**



**Notes**



**Did you stay sober today?**

☐ YES    ☐ NO

# Day _____ of my journey to a sober me!

| Date | Days sober |
|---|---|
|  |  |

**What are you grateful for today?**




**Steps I've taken today to ensure I stay sober**




### How did you feel today?

# 1  2  3  4  5  6  7  8  9  10

**Things I found hard today**




**Things I can do to help tomorrow...**




**Notes**




**Did you stay sober today?**

☐ YES   ☐ NO

# Day _____ of my journey to a sober me!

| Date | Days sober |
|---|---|
|  |  |

**What are you grateful for today?**

**Steps I've taken today to ensure I stay sober**

### How did you feel today?

1  2  3  4  5  6  7  8  9  10

**Things I found hard today**

**Things I can do to help tomorrow…**

**Notes**

**Did you stay sober today?**

☐ YES   ☐ NO

# Day _____ of my journey to a sober me!

| Date | Days sober |
|---|---|
|  |  |

**What are you grateful for today?**

**Steps I've taken today to ensure I stay sober**

### How did you feel today?

1   2   3   4   5   6   7   8   9   10

**Things I found hard today**

**Things I can do to help tomorrow…**

**Notes**

**Did you stay sober today?**

☐ YES  ☐ NO

# Day _____ of my journey to a sober me!

| Date | Days sober |
|---|---|
|  |  |

**What are you grateful for today?**

**Steps I've taken today to ensure I stay sober**

### How did you feel today?

1    2    3    4    5    6    7    8    9    10

**Things I found hard today**

**Things I can do to help tomorrow…**

**Notes**

**Did you stay sober today?**

☐ YES       ☐ NO

# Day _____ of my journey to a sober me!

| Date | Days sober |
|------|------------|

**What are you grateful for today?**

**Steps I've taken today to ensure I stay sober**

## How did you feel today?

# 1  2  3  4  5  6  7  8  9  10

**Things I found hard today**

**Things I can do to help tomorrow...**

**Notes**

**Did you stay sober today?**

☐ YES  ☐ NO

# Day _____ of my journey to a sober me!

| Date | Days sober |
|---|---|
|  |  |

**What are you grateful for today?**

**Steps I've taken today to ensure I stay sober**

## How did you feel today?

# 1  2  3  4  5  6  7  8  9  10

**Things I found hard today**

**Things I can do to help tomorrow...**

**Notes**

**Did you stay sober today?**

☐ **YES**        ☐ **NO**

# Day \_\_\_\_ of my journey to a sober me!

| Date | Days sober |
|---|---|
|  |  |

**What are you grateful for today?**

**Steps I've taken today to ensure I stay sober**

### How did you feel today?

1  2  3  4  5  6  7  8  9  10

**Things I found hard today**

**Things I can do to help tomorrow…**

**Notes**

**Did you stay sober today?**

☐ YES     ☐ NO

# Day _____ of my journey to a sober me!

| Date | Days sober |
|---|---|
| | |

**What are you grateful for today?**




**Steps I've taken today to ensure I stay sober**




### How did you feel today?

1  2  3  4  5  6  7  8  9  10

**Things I found hard today**




**Things I can do to help tomorrow...**




**Notes**




**Did you stay sober today?**

☐ YES      ☐ NO

# Day _____ of my journey to a sober me!

| Date | Days sober |
|------|------------|

**What are you grateful for today?**

**Steps I've taken today to ensure I stay sober**

## How did you feel today?

1  2  3  4  5  6  7  8  9  10

**Things I found hard today**

**Things I can do to help tomorrow...**

**Notes**

**Did you stay sober today?**

☐ YES     ☐ NO

# Day _____ of my journey to a sober me!

| Date | Days sober |
|---|---|
|  |  |

**What are you grateful for today?**

**Steps I've taken today to ensure I stay sober**

## How did you feel today?

1  2  3  4  5  6  7  8  9  10

**Things I found hard today**

**Things I can do to help tomorrow...**

**Notes**

**Did you stay sober today?**

☐ YES    ☐ NO

www.ingramcontent.com/pod-product-compliance
Lightning Source LLC
Chambersburg PA
CBHW071403080526
44587CB00017B/3165